6 95
BFT

Books By
NANCY SIRKIS

NEWPORT:
Pleasures and Palaces

BOSTON

ONE FAMILY

ONE
FAMILY

ONE FAMILY

text and
photographs by

NANCY SIRKIS

introduction by

Julian Bond

LITTLE, BROWN AND COMPANY
Boston / Toronto

Library of Congress Catalog Card No.
73-121425
 JUL 26 '71
01309 W0601 T11/70

First Edition

Published simultaneously in Canada by
Little, Brown & Company (Canada) Limited

Printed in the United States of America

For Linda,
Kim, Michael,
Michelle, Greta,
Joe, Corina,
Nat, Ulysses,
La Frances, Andrew
and Daniel

Introduction

Nancy Sirkis' *One Family* gives the reader a look he may not want at the life lived by the Black family — the mother, Mrs. Frances Black, and her ten children.

Their life is a typical one for Welfare families. Typical except that Mrs. Black has so far refused to let the system crush her down.

One Family is both Mrs. Black's family and all families, then. What is different here is that Mrs. Black makes herself come alive, makes her problems common ones that any head of household must face at one time or another.

Those who purchase this book, however, may not have to buy the cheapest possible clothes for their children; may not have to stay at home because working means losing income, not gaining it; may not have to buy food for their families every other day instead of every week or two.

There is no strident argument here that America's Welfare system is wrong and criminal; *One Family* demonstrates that it is without argument, without anything more than Mrs. Black's words, her children's thoughts, and Nancy Sirkis' sensitive photographs.

Mrs. Black sums it up best: "Whether you have the don't care attitude, or whether you have the I care attitude, you still don't get what you want. Care or don't, you still the same. You still got no money. You still got no food. So what's the difference if you care or don't care? That don't put money in your pocket or food in your mouth."

Julian Bond
August 11, 1970

Preface

It was not by accident that I, a middle-class New Yorker, met and became friendly with Mrs. Frances Black, a Welfare mother who had borne fourteen children.

Under ordinary circumstances, Mrs. Black would have been a statistic to me, one of the one-out-of-eight New Yorkers who, according to Mayor Lindsay, by the end of 1969 would be on Welfare. For Mrs. Black, I might have been a nameless "whitey," since the two of us and our families live three blocks apart on New York's West Side — three very long blocks that separate middle-class Riverside Drive from the city housing projects on Columbus Avenue. But as a photographer I had been engaged on a self-assigned photo essay on women; as a mother of one child I had become very interested in photographing a woman who was faced with the enormous task of raising a great many children by herself. I searched my neighborhood for such a woman. She had to be intelligent, personable, and with a family that was still functioning as a unit.

As my inquiry progressed, Mrs. Black's name kept being mentioned by women who knew her. (I knew many neighborhood mothers through an interracial neighborhood group that my own son attended.) She had no telephone, so I wrote her a note stating that I was a photographer and would come by to see her about a photographic project that I was working on.

Of course, the day that I did ring the doorbell, Mrs. Black did not want to let me in. She thought that I was an investigator for Welfare. (No matter how old my dungarees were, it was always assumed by Mrs. Black's neighbors, the other housing project tenants, that I was either a visiting nurse, or took care of children for a sick mother, or was an investigator. Nobody harbored any illusions that I lived in the project.)

I explained to Mrs. Black my interest in doing a photo essay on women, and that I wanted her story to be a part of it. I could not guarantee her any money, but if I did sell the pictures, I promised her a share of the proceeds. However, our original agreement promised her only a beautiful set of photographs of her family.

Mrs. Black agreed, and we set a date to begin shooting. When I came back to start, Mrs. Black answered the door. But she had forgotten about the date and didn't feel like having pictures taken. So we just sat and talked.

Many times when I came to take pictures we just talked. I don't remember now what our early conversations were about—just two women talking. Gradually I began taking pictures. Since I had always arrived with a camera (a single Nikon with an extra lens), the children accepted the camera as part of me and didn't pay too much attention when I actually began to use it.

In time—these photographs were taken off and on over a period of just over one and a half years—it became clear that the story I was shooting was not just about a woman with many children, but about a particular Welfare mother trying to raise a family under the Welfare system. This then, became the story — the story of one of the most urgent unsolved problems facing our country, the story of a mother trying to survive against terrible odds in a world of Welfare that few people understand and almost all condemn.

For Mrs. Black and myself, the turning point came in the course of a conversation when we discovered that we were the same age. I had assumed she was older; she had assumed I was younger. At that moment the gulf between our two worlds was revealed at its widest: she with fourteen children and little hope for the future; I with one child, a husband, and attainable dreams. We sat in silence facing each other — two people, one white, one black; one richer, one poorer — two women.

———————————————

Mrs. Frances Black (which is, by the way, her real name) was born in Screven, Georgia, on February 6, 1937. Her childhood was spent in Tillman, South Carolina, where she was raised by an aunt, Lillie Mae, whom she always refers to as her mother. Her education was interrupted in the ninth grade by her marriage to a young lumber worker. She was then fourteen years old. By nineteen, she had four daughters.

Leaving her daughters with relatives in the South ("I don't know why, I just left — wasn't no work or anything"), she came to New York City alone. She had relatives in Manhattan, and as a child had visited them with her aunt. Shortly after arriving, she took a sleep-in maid's job, but quit after three months. It was too much work for too little money. Then children began arriving on an all too regular basis.

Today, her family consists of the four daughters who live with relatives, and the ten children whom she herself is raising. Those living with her are Linda, thirteen; Kim, eleven; the twins Michael and Michelle, nine; Greta, eight; Joe, seven; Corina, six; Nat, five; Ulysses ("Poopie"), three; and the baby, La Frances, two, who was born with brain damage which Mrs. Black attributes to a difficult labor. There is also one grandchild by her eldest daughter Helen, who has moved to New York and occasionally visits her. About ten years ago, Mrs. Black was added to the city's Welfare rolls.

In 1967, Mrs. Black was living at 13 West 103rd Street, in four roach- and mice-infested rooms. She had nine children and was pregnant with La Frances. Because the apartment was hopelessly overcrowded and mice-ridden, Mrs. Black wrote to the authorities and pleaded with her investigator for better housing. Nothing happened.

Eventually, large with child and with nine children in tow, Mrs. Black went down to the office of Percy Sutton, then president of the Borough of Manhattan, to demonstrate for a decent place to live. The demonstration received a great deal of publicity, and Mrs. Black blames many of her present problems on that publicity. However, it did get her a five-room apartment in a city housing project at 103rd Street and Columbus Avenue. It was to be temporary quarters until a large project in the Polo Grounds was completed, where she was to be allocated an eight-room apartment.

From the day I met her, she and her children spoke constantly of moving into the Polo Grounds, as if by moving there all of their problems would be solved. But when the Polo Grounds project was completed, there was no apartment there for her. A year later, she and her family were moved to her present six-room apartment in a different building in the same Columbus Avenue project.

16

In this, her present apartment, life once again became intolerable for Mrs. Black. She claims that someone obtained the publicity about her demonstrating for an apartment and circulated it among the tenants of the project. Subsequently her children were teased and the knocking on her door in the early hours of the morning began.

Today, after the recent cuts in Welfare checks by the state and city of New York, Mrs. Black receives $256 every two weeks to feed, clothe and care for herself and her ten children. This allows about $1.66 per day for each member of the family to live on; rent is paid separately by additional checks of $53.50 twice a month. To exist on this allotment Mrs. Black would have to operate with severe budgetary efficiency, taking advantage of every food sale, buying her clothes at the end of each season, and not allowing her children candy, ice cream or carfare.

In any human circumstances, this would be difficult; in Mrs. Black's circumstances it is impossible.

First, Mrs. Black never has enough money on hand to buy economically, so the small rather than the economy size package is bought. Lack of a large freezer eliminates meat sales. The cheap clothing tears and becomes unwearable shortly after purchase; nothing lasts long enough to become a hand-me-down. With ten children, the cheap furniture must often be replaced. The current bed frames, which are broken, lasted only one year, and the mattresses are soaked with urine, for the furniture allotment did not allow for rubber sheets. Finally, Mrs. Black's work in caring for ten children is so enormous that expensive shortcuts are taken: the baby uses disposable diapers, the children's shirts are occasionally sent out to the Chinese laundry, and the food is purchased day-to-day at a small neighborhood store that offers credit, rather than at the supermarket which doesn't. The children are constantly sent out for things, and as children will, if they have cash in hand, they spend the leftover change on sweets.

As a result of all this, Mrs. Black finds that she often runs out of food money towards the end of the second week. Money that should be spent on clothes is then spent on food, and the result is that the children must sometimes stay home from school because of lack of clothing. Last winter several of the children regularly could not go to school on very cold days because they did not own winter coats.

From the day I met Mrs. Black, she spoke of wanting to go to work. Time after time she requested money for baby-sitters from her investigator so that she could take a job. She felt that a healthy woman should work, that she would feel better leaving the house each morning to work rather than sitting and waiting for a Welfare check. I don't believe she realized, or wanted to realize, that working would not substantially increase her income, and that the net result would only be a reduction in her Welfare check. The investigator, of course, informed her that there was no baby-sitting money available. Day care centers are available for a mother with two or three children, but with ten children Mrs. Black was apparently out of luck. "They didn't give me no reason why I couldn't leave my children in a center," she said later. "There was a long waiting list. They just give me the runaround."

While I was finishing this book, Mrs. Black entered a New York Telephone Company training program. She had not found a solution to the baby-sitting problem; sometimes Linda baby-sits, sometimes there is no one to sit and she never gets to the training program.

To an observer, one of the most immediately apparent aspects of project living is the strong motivation to "keep up with the Joneses" that exists. The children look out of their windows and check to see whose windows have curtains— and a great deal of effort goes into keeping up the windows in the project. Mrs. Black's children were teased because their windows were bare. However, the Black family living room is well furnished and maintained; as Mrs. Black often indicated, when one has so little, one is ashamed to show it. There is also a dining table, but it is rarely used; the chairs are tipped upside down on top of it, as in a restaurant.

The project building is relatively well maintained; certainly it is much better than the tenements in which most of the tenants existed previously. However, as another tenant explained to me, there seems to be a relatively short period before any low-income housing project building becomes inundated with the odors of stale cooking and urine. This building was no exception. Once, someone vomited on the elevator door and the tenants and I looked at the vomit for two weeks before it was cleaned off. There were also many muggings and rapes in the building; I was warned not to get into the elevator with any man I did not know.

After I had decided to try to report Mrs. Black's story, she and I had conversations on many subjects: Welfare, living on Welfare allowances, why she had so many children, the demonstration, living in city housing projects, what she wants for herself and her children, what the children wanted, and so on. Everything was recorded on tapes. In transcribing the tapes I tried to capture the sound of the family as it is—pronunciation, sentence structure, and all. The text in this book is by the family, except the notes in parentheses which are mine. After finishing, I had Mrs. Black read and approve everything that she and her family said, for I want this story to be theirs.

Mrs. Black talking about herself

I was born in Screven, Georgia.
Grew up in Tillman, South Carolina,
till I got married. Well I was raised
there an I loved it. I was small, lots of
cousins, aunts and uncles. Moved to
the city thirteen years ago. I had
folks up here. I used to go to school
here, visiting on vacations from six
on . . . my aunt, uncles. I like the city.

My mother, I don't even think that
I could be like my mother. She was
strict, but not too strict. She was very
good. I don't know but some of it
should rub off on me. I don't take my
kids like my mother used to take us to
different things . . . places you know,
she wouldn't go many places unless
she take me. I can't do that. I can't
do that. I don't have enough money.
I have too many children. See, I
can't do it.

My real mother didn't raise me. My
aunt raised me, but I call her my
mother. My real mother, Mamie Lee,
only have one child and Lillie Mae,
she raised three. She have two other
children, but anyway she raised me.
There's no particular reason, it's just
she wanted a child.

In the South I never did go out that
much. I never did, you know. I
played around out in our yard. Very
seldom I got to go out. But we go to

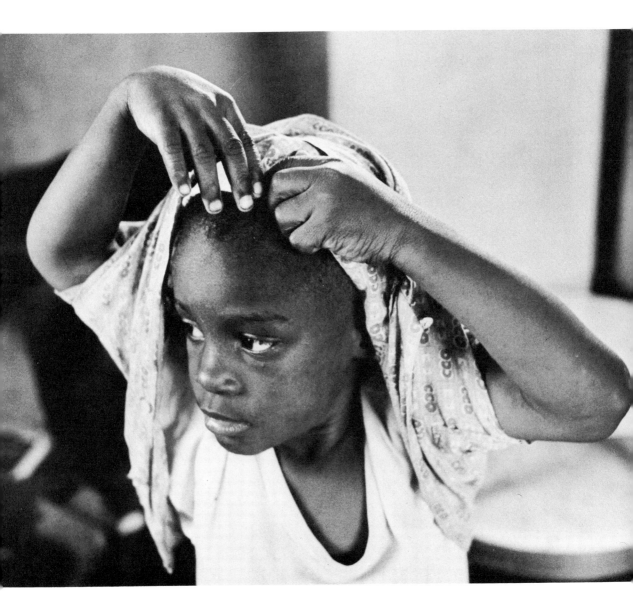

church all the time, you know. All through the week an on Sunday.

I told Linda [the thirteen-year-old] when I was goin to school down South, it seemed like we learned much more. Today the children not too interested in goin to school. Too many other things are attractive to them. I never did stay out when I was a child. I never did cause my mother did make me go to bed—not make me, cause I know the time to go to bed, round about seven-thirty. Sometimes on the weekend, I might stay up till bout eleven.

Up here it's very hard to keep your children in the house—even if you have to. Cause what's goin on outside is temptation. I guess so much things looks good, better than it does in the home. I have nothin here that attracts the children, that makes them stay at home. Cause the rules an regulations that the parents has is good. But so much goin on outside that they stays outside an don't obey them.

Yeh, I can do somethin about Linda. Linda will say she goin out to the [neighborhood] Center, cause Center supposed to be havin parties; an they do give parties. But they go out an stay after the party. This is an excuse, you know. It's an excuse for Linda. She say: "I'm goin to the party." So naturally I say yes. So from the party she goes back with them. Yeh, it worries me. Kim don't do that like Linda. Kim sometimes come home. She know. Sometimes Kim with Linda, she bad. Most of the time she possibly here.

I'm bout the same as she is, my mother [Lillie Mae]. She probably have more patience than I have. She had a lot to do. Like I said, she had a motel, you know, something like a hotel back here. They had a lot to do with the public, so she had a lot to do. We had a big house and a little house. The big house was the boarding house. We had roomers there. We had the little house by ourselves. It really was a good town. I had a room of my own. Everything was better than it is now.

They both raised me. My uncle is dead, so I don't talk too much about him. Sure he was good. My uncle was very nice. I called him my father too. Sometimes I believed that he loved me even more than she do. He took me to church. My mother, she believed in prayer a lot. She liked church, but most of the time she stayed an took care of the business. My uncle, everywhere he went, I went with him.

I just haven't gotten out to goin to church around here. I sound like I'm

condemning the churches, but I'm not like that. I don't condemn all of them; but if I did go to church, it would be a certain kind of church I would go to — a Protestant Holiness Church, a sanctified church.

Well, it was very good, you know. She was strict, but not too strict. My whole life, my whole childhood, was good up until I got married when I was fourteen.

After I got married, I started havin children up till the time I come up here. I was nineteen when I come up here, an kids weren't with me then. Helen [Mrs. Black's eldest] is up here now. The rest is with relatives. Haven't seen them since they were babies. They all in school. They doin good.

I had a sleep-in job when I first come to New York. I worked about three months. I didn't like it. It wasn't payin me much. Then I got on Welfare.

Well, I been married for eighteen years, never been divorced, just separated. I'm still married. I have fourteen kids. I raised most of them. Helen was raised by my mother till she moved to here. Then I have the other three. Their grandmother haves one. My aunt has one. Another relative has the other. They

eighteen, sixteen, fourteen and ten.
I don't see them much. The rest I
raised by myself.

I didn't sit down an plan nothin. I
never thought of havin children, but
once I had em, they're mine. I've
never prevented havin children. I
just never planned, if I got pregnant I
just had the baby — simple as that.
The government wasn't quite so bold
as they are now. About eight years
ago, I just find out [about birth
control]. I just didn't use it. When I
did start, I didn't like it.

It was easier raising them down
South. I don't know, to me it's
crowded here — cold. Like where I
was born there wasn't too many
people. We had certain hours to go
to bed. We didn't go to other
people's houses. Wasn't like this.
Couldn't hardly do that here. You
can lay down laws. Can't get the kids
to obey. It's more interesting out
there [outside] than whatever I have
at home. Those things must be more
fascinatin than what I keep my
children in.

The older ones look after the smaller
ones. They're playful. They got
things out there I don't have in here
for sure. They have things that they
play with out there. The streets has a
great influence on them, especially

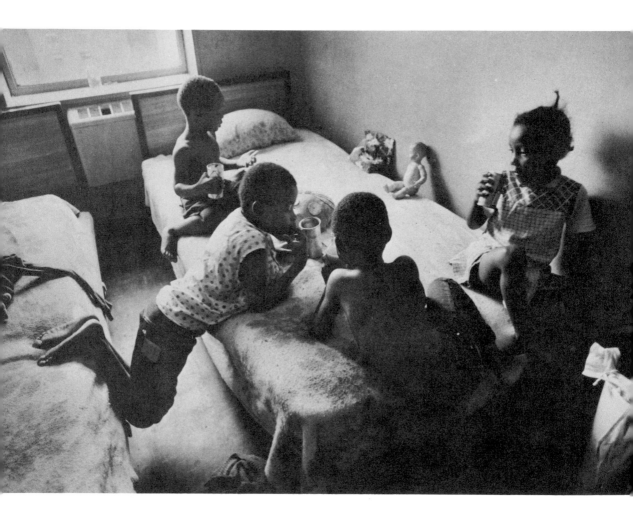

the bigger children. You all know what's goin on out there.

You tell Kim, if I catch her smokin cigarettes, I'm gonna make her eat the whole package.

Sometimes some of the other kids around take money from them. They get beat up. Michelle almost cried to keep from goin down there one time. They meet them out there and beat them up an take money. I guess all of them's bad, mine and everybody else's. I don't know, I thinks it's more easy to be bad than to be good.

Kim was almost raped about three weeks ago. She ran out an we went to catch who did it. She came in with her hair all up over her head, like she woke up this morning. An her heart was beating real fast. She was, you know, like cryin.

They didn't want to go outside, cause I tell them they have to go. They can't just stay in the house all the time. They used to go to group durin the summer. Not now. They haven't started comin yet — this summer thing. [This was in July.]

They go out, some of them sometimes. But when it's bad weather I don't let them go out every day. Well, I don't think that I want them out anyway; what can happen to Kim. I was afraid to let them go out, one by one, especially the girls.

I want them to look nice. I think it's a natural thing for kids to look nice. I don't care what category you fall in. I don't want them to look no better than how they livin. Why should I make them dressed up when I'm not able to afford it? But I want whatever they got on to be clean. I want it to be nice. Yes, I want them to have nice things on. I want to see that it's clean. Yeh, I'm very fussy about that.

I don't know how other people is bein treated. I only can say what I'm goin through. I don't know what's happenin to everybody. I'm telling you what's happenin to me an my children. I don't know nobody in this building. You can get "clean": I mean you can get dressed up — the black man say you can get "clean." When you get ready, you can buy clothes. But there are other people who can go out an put on their jeans an that's probably all they got. So you know you got somethin to wear when you go home an want to come back an look sharp. But suppose I go out there. That may be all I got. But they knows that you's got somethin else. Linda knows why she should be nice, cause they tease Linda about the way she dressed.

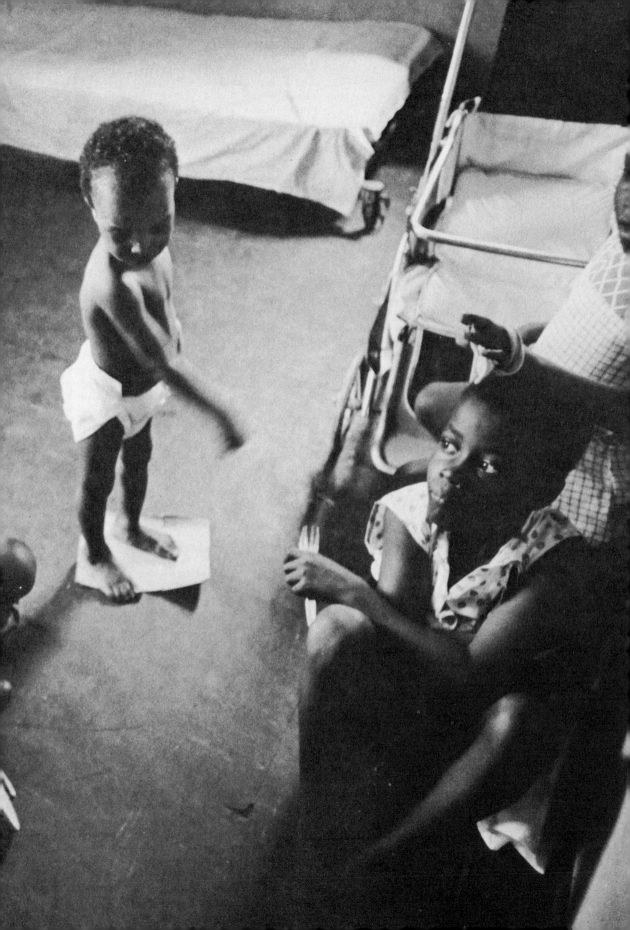

Mrs. Black at the housing demonstration

Well, bein the time I demonstrated . . .
I demonstrated because I was livin
in a four-room apartment with nine
kids. 103rd Street, 13 West 103rd
Street, I was livin. It was too hard
against me, that's why I had to move.
You know, the mice. The place was
infested with all kinds of pests — I
don't know, I was bitten by a mouse
an two of them was on the baby. Not
rats, but there were mice, an I had
to kick them off cause he was gettin
down an eatin away, knawin away
on my feet. An I had to kick him off
before he get and jumped off the bed.

I went down to the housing, I went
down several years before they sent
for me, but I didn't get help. But then
I asked several times if I was gonna
get on the list. Then they finally
wrote a letter, not exactly stating that
I was ineligible, but it all meant the
same thing — I'm sorry that your family
are . . . the composition of family
doesn't stand up to our rules and
regulations.

I went to Percy Sutton's office to
demonstrate. We was with different
organizations, an all the children.
We was on TV, radio an the news.
All nine children; at the time I was
pregnant with Frances.

Overleaf: Mrs. Black and her children: on the windowsill is Ulysses ("Poopie"); on the back of the couch are Nat and Corina; on the couch from left to right are Joe, Greta, Michelle, Mrs. Black with La Frances, Linda, and Michael; on the floor is Kim.

Well, we just sit there. They were very nice people, I hate to admit, but true. Sutton was very nice. I talked to him. But first another guy, he was very rude in the beginning. He calmed down. But Mr. Sutton, he was very nice. First he claimed that this was a joke; I wasn't for real. But then they found out we wasn't leavin. Then this other guy — about three minutes later he come, and unfortunately he was very rude and said something about why we come from the slums and come up there botherin him. So anyway, we stay there for hours and finally Mr. Sutton spoke to me over the phone from Chicago. He was very, very nice to me.

Then they made arrangements that we get . . . you know . . . gave all the demonstrators food, gave my baby milk, things to eat, diapers. I mean he was very wonderful. But then after the demonstration I moved here. They promised it to me right away, I moved here one year ago.

Things weren't happening so bad to me at that particular time. They make the sly remarks. They only put me here temporarily till the polo grounds got built. They promised me first priority on the polo grounds.

This is the whole thing. We demonstrated to get an apartment. An when the polo grounds built, there I was supposed to go. So, when the polo grounds was completed, I was gonna get an apartment there. I didn't. Well, well, the then former President . . . Johnson . . . it was told to me that he had the polo grounds, the larger apartments reserved for the families that was in areas like in the Bronx. An he reserved them for Model Cities. But anyway, it was for the poor.

You have to get a good reason to get in the projects. You certainly wouldn't want to move out of a good place to move into the projects. You have to live in a place that was awful an bad to want to live in the projects in the first place.

I think that you have to have good reasons for livin in the projects. I don't know about these coops an stuff now. If you got the money — good. I think you have to have a pretty good reason, because I don't think they give a person if he's got six rooms an it's nice. They're not eligible for the project.

The people out there in what we call Model Cities, they really needed an apartment, as the places where they lived must of been terrible. It's reserved for those families.

The second reason, cause they say
my place is too small, overcrowded.
Since I couldn't move to the polo
grounds, they gave me a project here.

Well, I don't like it so well. Not now.
Because the incidents that I have, as
well as the children. Because of the
demonstration I suppose. Our place
was over-occupied. The city told
me that I would have to move. So
that was the second reason that I have
to move. I wouldn't mind it if some
of the tenants weren't giving me a
hard time. An it's not so good for my
children.

Well, during the time that I
demonstrated . . . Once you
publicized, an you still in the same
place, it's bad for you an your

children. It bothers you, you know.
Everybody knows you. The children
would tease my children. Even in
school they would have a pretty hard
time. They can't go down to play.
The children would always beat them
up. Then they tease them about
things that happen at Sutton's office
sayin, "No more rats from Mrs.
Black." Then my children get beat
up in the elevator.

I think once you publicized, an once
the kids know, they always pick on
you. All I know is what's happening
to me.

This is how I feel, an this is what I
know. I know that them teasin the
kids bout how they got in, cryin,
sayin, "No more rats from Mrs.
Black," an all the sort of slogans that
they use that they mentioned from
goin to Sutton's office. There they
used to have the little leaflets that
they would have for people to read
about almost a year later. I found all
those leaflets distributed over the
place. See, my older daughter almost
got in a fight about it, an she cried
too, cause it hurt her. So I been goin
through it since I been here.

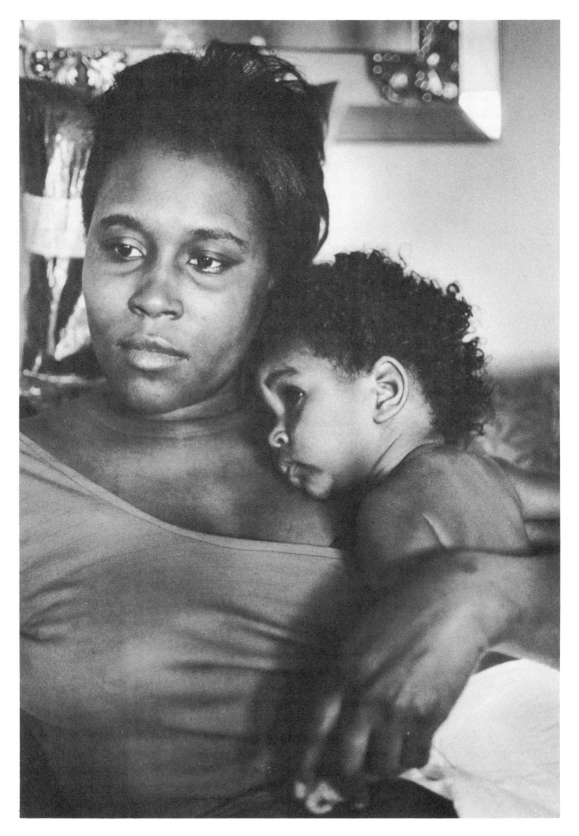

Mrs. Black on the noises

Well, I've lost quite a bit of weight
since this knockin an everything.
Cause I've gotten to the point that I
can't sleep.

Well, first it started with somebody
bangin the door. First it started, it
seemed like it was durin the day.
Then it was durin the night. Then the
whole time, night an day. They been
doin that about three months. It's
some kind of knockin, like somebody
breakin in.

Then I went to the cops an report it.
It was all durin the day and night
continuously. That's why I went to
the cops, the police. Nobody could
catch them.

They stop for a while. Then, it was
over a month ago, they started again,
louder than they was before. An
then they start like four o'clock in the
mornin. Lasts sometimes till about
eight o'clock. An then I can't go
back to sleep cause I have to get up
and go to work, you know.
Without sleep I be sick an then I have
to go to work not feelin well. Then it
wakes up my children — have them
nervous also. You don't know when
to expect them. You know they
comin, an we know they comin
round about the same time. But

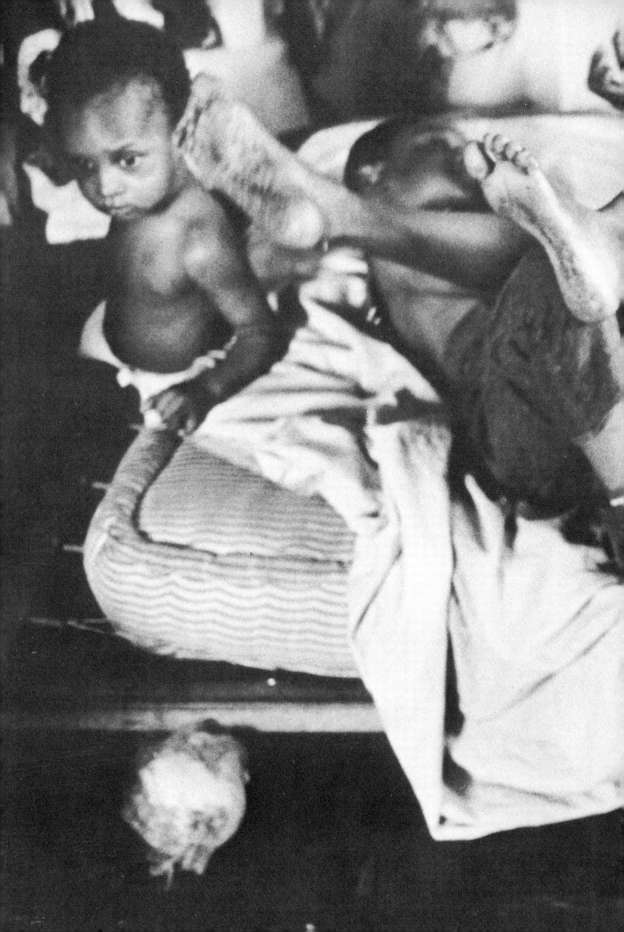

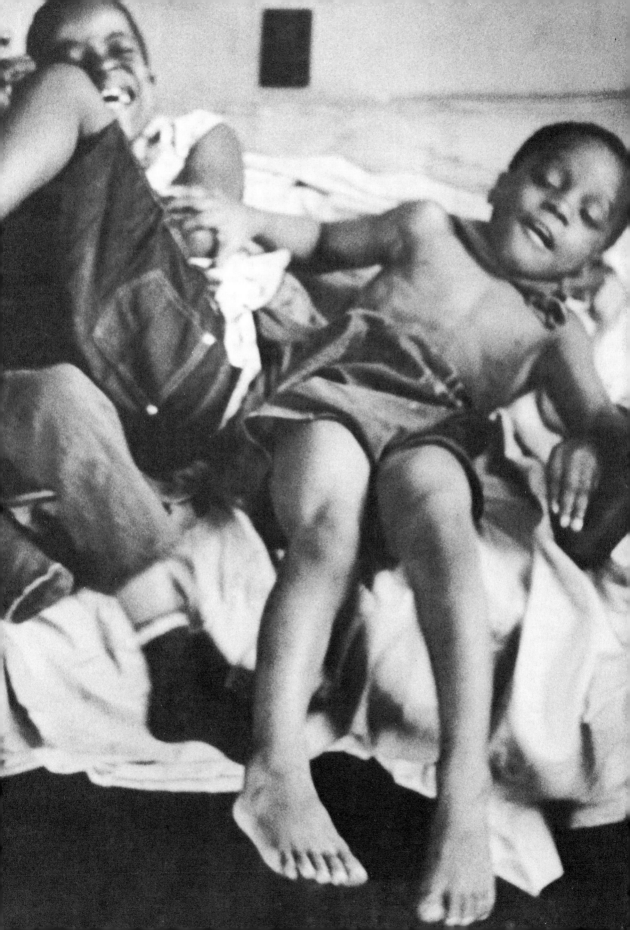

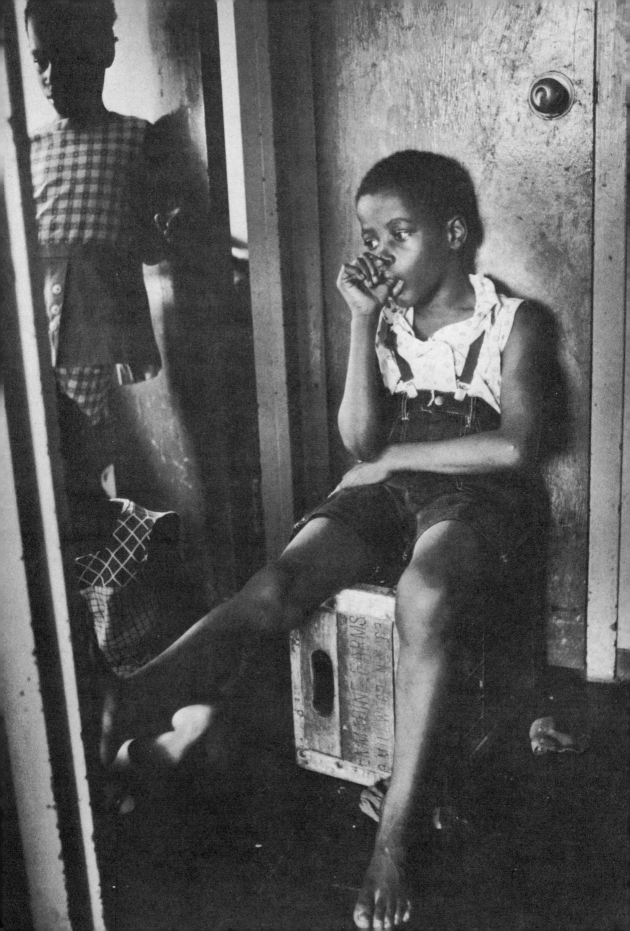

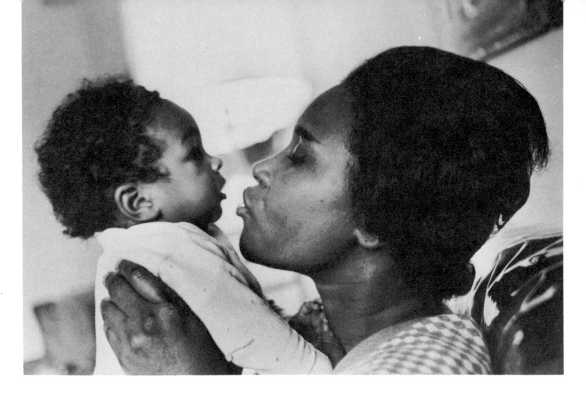

you never can get used to that sort of noise. Cause every time you go to sleep, you know you gonna wake up an you can't go back to sleep.

I don't know about the other people, but like I tol you, I know what I'm experiencing. There's a tenants' council, but there's not many people in the tenants' council. . . . I don't know, I don't have the answer. I have gone to tenants' council meetings, but they're just a handful, comparin to the thousands of people that lives here. But they haves a tenants' patrol here from maybe six or seven in the evening till bout ten, eleven maybe the latest.

But after the knockin, this ol lady beats on the drum, least that what it sound like. Then, one morning we

got up an there was such a noise that the children, everybody woked up an started runnin toward the front door. We all sat down in here an Linda said, "You know, it's smokin in here." We looked outside. You know, smoke comin all through the cracks of the door. An we open the door, and there was all the stuff they had set fire to.

After then, they took the lock off the door. What you call the little round thing, the cylinder or something? They took that off the door.

The children would get beat up. I sayin that again. Once you publicized an your kids picked out, they always doin somethin to your kids. No, you wouldn't understand cause it's not happenin to you.

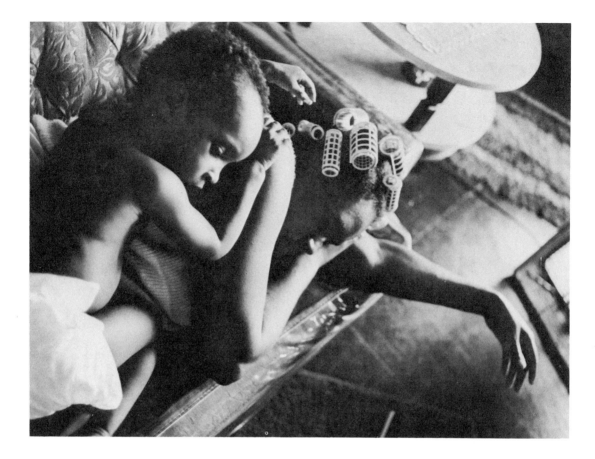

La Frances

Mrs. Black speaking about Welfare

It's horrible to live on Welfare. I just came on Welfare about ten years ago. I just got on — that's all. Well, I tell you bein on Welfare was pretty tough. Because like trying to get an apartment an you tell them how many children you got. But the bad thing about it: when you tell them you on Welfare, it's hard to get anything. If you get an apartment, you have to tell your means of support — particularly in order to get an apartment. You have to tell how much you make. How you gonna pay the rent. When you tell them, "Welfare," they slam the phone down. The place I found was all filled with Welfare. I was at 84th Street at the time.

When you on Welfare, you always somewhat different. Because you getting public assistance, you know you don't work. You read on the back of the checks what it really say. I always read the back of it. [The following is printed on the back of Welfare checks: "By endorsing or cashing this check I state that I and members of my family whose support is included in this check are destitute and still in need of public assistance . . . ."]

You are different. I know, because we are human being, I know it's our world too. Poor man is in one category, an Welfare recipients. When you in Welfare, even the poorest looks down.

It would be nice if I could work an make enough money for these children . . . which may be impossible if I could make enough.

They [the Welfare Department] don't want you to have nothing, a telephone, not anything. These thing are a luxury. To get simple things becomes a fight. I had an investigator. She lied. She said I'm gonna send money up for coats. I said to her where's the money for the coats, we're not getting them. An she said no.

One time I take all the children downtown an threaten to leave them.

They are cruel some of them [caseworkers], very nasty. I've met many that give me the things that I asked for; an some that they saw what I really needed an still wouldn't give. They make you feel lower than you really feel. They know that you destitute. That's one of the words on the back of the check, that you destitute; that you need public assistance, that you have no other means of support; an naturally, you different.

They're superior, the investigators. When you bein the one that's asking . . . if I don't have anything an you have to give me something all the time. If you get because you need it, when a person needs something all the time an have to ask — that means the one that's givin is superior.

You can't hardly do nothin with a little bit of money. I can't but buy a little bit. I do big shopping every two weeks, when the check comes. I usually spends thirty-five to forty dollars but every day I buy. We have to buy milk an bread. Goin on the second week I run out of money. When I don't borrow nothin, sometimes we go hungry.

I used to cook all the time, macaroni an potato salad any time of day or night; but Welfare don't expect you to eat like that.

If I feeds the kids there isn't money for clothes. They eats vegetables every day. But there's a lot of starchy foods. We get more canned goods than we do meat. If I had a freezer I wouldn't have to go to the store every day. Buyin every day costs more.

They likes cereal. I'm not able to buy it every day. They uses too much milk. All this week they been eatin corn flakes an milk. That's what I been buyin.

When they go to school, I have to
buy them the necessities what they
need most. If Michael got pants I
don't buy him some, I buy somebody
else. If they don't have clothes they
stay home till I get some money.

First time Mr. S. [an official from the
Welfare Department] came by, he
told me to give some of my kids away.

I don't have the money. Like I want
to take my children downtown to see
a play. My mother used to take me.
Like when we used to come up here,
she would take me to Radio City an
you know in Harlem . . . we'd go to
the Apollo.

I need linens, forks, plates, spreads,
curtains, curtain rods, an clothes,
an jewelry, an beds. The beds broke
up, the mattresses all wet up. I
bought beds twice in three years.

The children don't like the idea of
me bein on Welfare. I could be off
Welfare an they would like it much
more. The other children tease them
about bein on Welfare. I don't know
why, I don't know why.

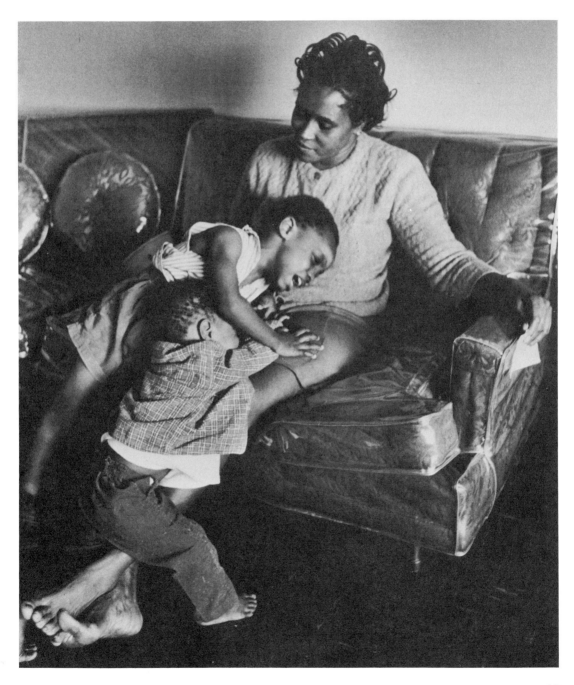

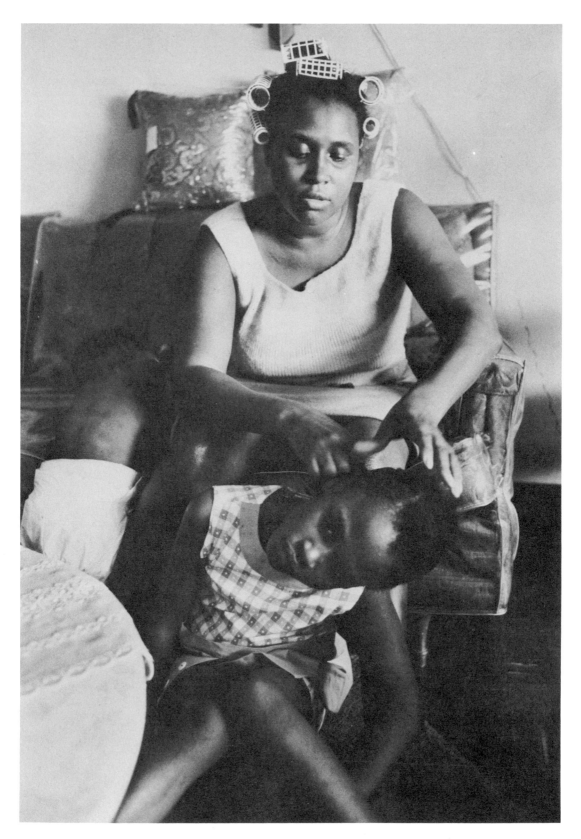

Mrs. Black talking
about respect and work

I don't know about this building, but
I thought it had been kept nice.
Well, see, I'm gonna tell you the
difference between people. Doctors
or not, you know, but the atmosphere
is different. You can walk right on the
street, come off the avenue, it's just
like two different places. The place is
quiet there on the street, and no
children or whole lot of noises. Right
on the avenue, it's the noises; it's
everything you catch.

Well, some people, you know, they
can't have what they want an they
can't get what they want. You know
there's sometimes they don't care a
thing. It's the attitude that you get.
But still, in the meantime, you got a
reason for havin that don't care
attitude. Whether you have the don't
care attitude, or whether you have
the I care attitude, you still don't get
what you want. Care or don't, you
still the same. You still got no money.
You still got no food. So what's the
difference if you care or don't care?
That don't put money in your pocket
or food in your mouth.

When you depressed, well it's natural
to feel that way. That's why I say you

have a reason. Psychologically speakin, it does make it worse. But actually it don't make it no worse, cause whether you care or not care, you still poor. Far as doin anything, it doesn't put money in my pocket.

This apartment could be kept nice an clean. But heck, it's so bad lookin. So you look at the same ragged stuff all day long. You don't care.

It does matter to them, cause kids tease them about their house, how the house look. No doubt some of these kids has worse.

I have gotten a feelin about don't care. I think many people feels it. Whether they rich or poor. I always try for somethin fine.

I could be the poorest people in the world, I know me, I don't want to sit an wait on Welfare. I would of worked long time ago if I have somebody to baby-sit, you know.

Workin don't kill nobody. It's a helpful thing to get out every day. You know, I feel much better to go out. [Mrs. Black is in a training program to become a long-distance telephone operator.] Nothin wrong with workin. I see nothin wrong with workin, I think that's the plan from the beginning. There's nothin wrong with a woman workin.

But seem some people, I guess many people feel cause I can get as much on Welfare. You only get fifty dollars pay an you have to pay the baby-sitter an you end up with nothin. You have to have carfare. You have nothin. Am I right? So you may as well stay home.

But I don't have that attitude. You know, if I make fifteen dollars profit, it's mine. I feel worthful. It's a feeling I have like God bless me for helpin friends. I like to go out there while I got the courage . . . go out there an earn a little somethin.

I love these little children. I love bein with them, but still, it would feel good to work. You see, I bein with my kids all their lives, so I don't mind. Just workin is a new thing. I've always been with them, but to go out an work, I think it's a healthy thing.

Workin or not workin . . . I don't know. If you a good person, or if you nice — I consider myself nice an I carry myself in that way — you get respect an what-not, you know, workin or not workin. You give respect an you get it. It doesn't matter, you sit down with friends. We talked before an we still talk. It's just that now I tells them things that go on on the job. We have somethin different to talk about, that's the only thing.

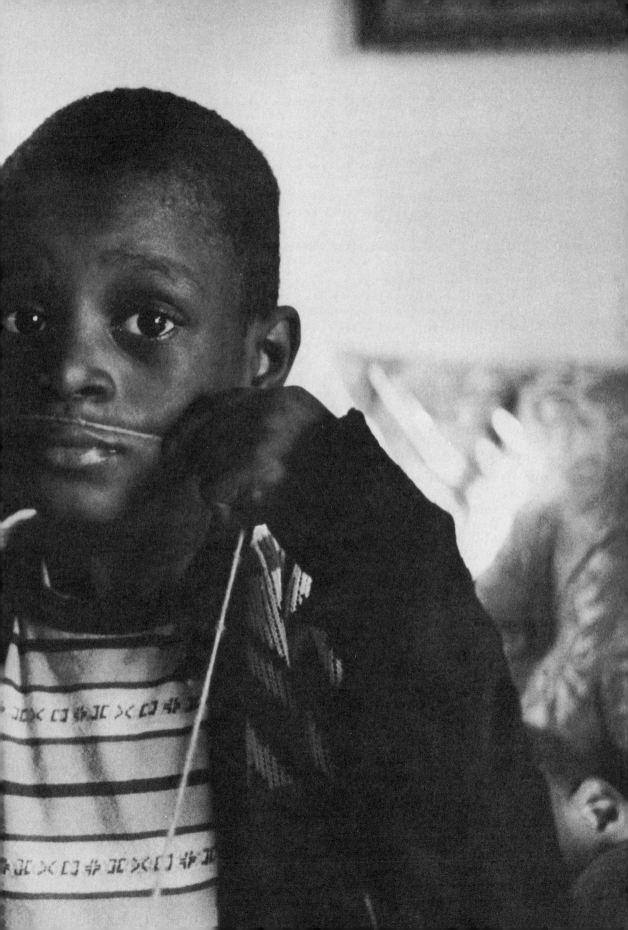

Sure I can get up things that I wanted. Yes, I certainly do feels much better. You know, I feel real independent. This is what I'm talking about. It's good for you to work. It's a healthy thing. You can wash dishes. An in a way there's nothin wrong with bein on Welfare. But, I feel like if you healthy an can get a job, I thinks it's wonderful if you can work.

I couldn't earn enough, that's almost impossible. I dont' know, because I still be getting help when you independent. You know what I mean. I don't think many of the people on Welfare, I mean ordinary people, don't make enough to live off, let alone me an my kinfolk. But it still give a great deal of satisfaction just to go out an work.

I'm trying to work cause my check was cut an you know it takes a lot to live with these children. These children, I got many of them, food alone costs, not to mention their clothing. They have to have haircuts. You know, they have different places that they go to. It costs money for everything. It would take more money than I'm getting now, that's for sure.

I told them I was goin to work, so nothin will happen when they find out. I don't care if they lower the check. I'm still gonna work. I feel much better since I work.

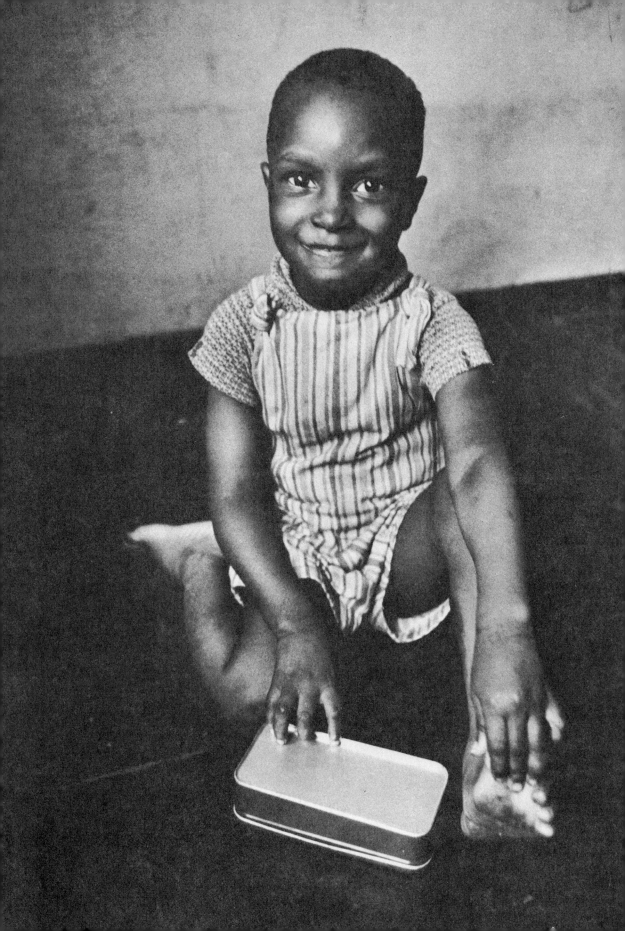

Ulysses

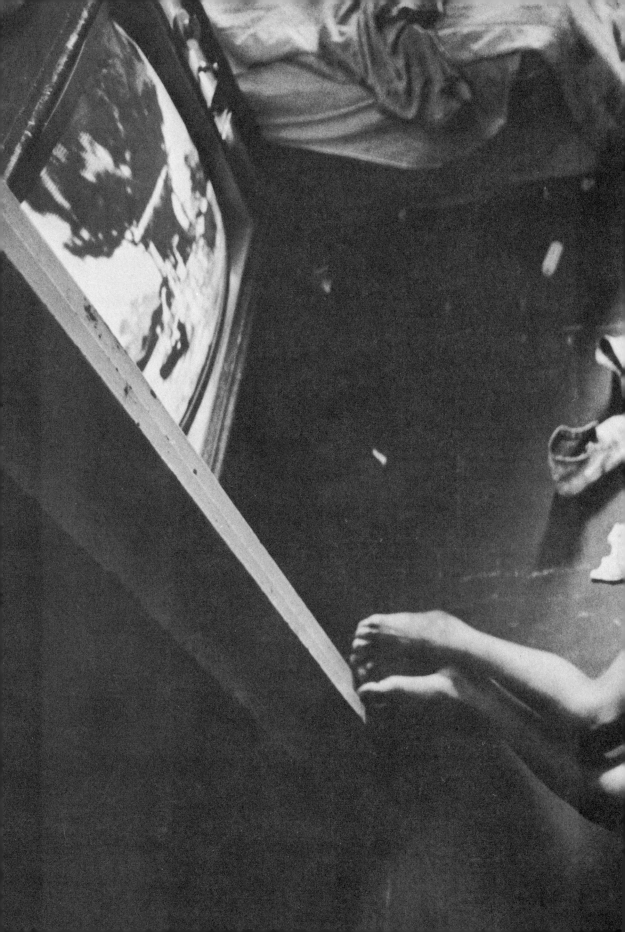

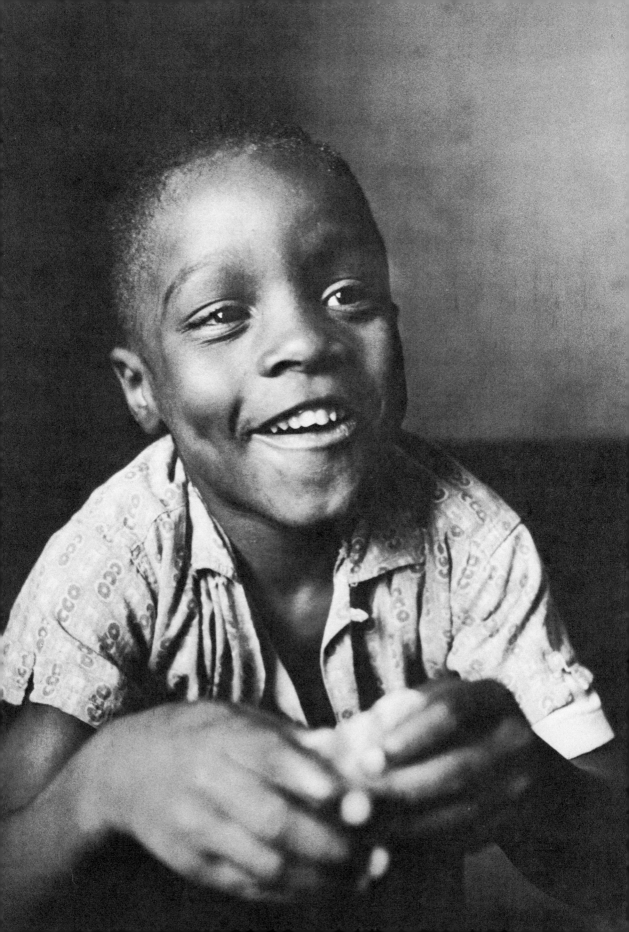

NAT–five years old

I want to be a fire[man], cause to stop
the fires.

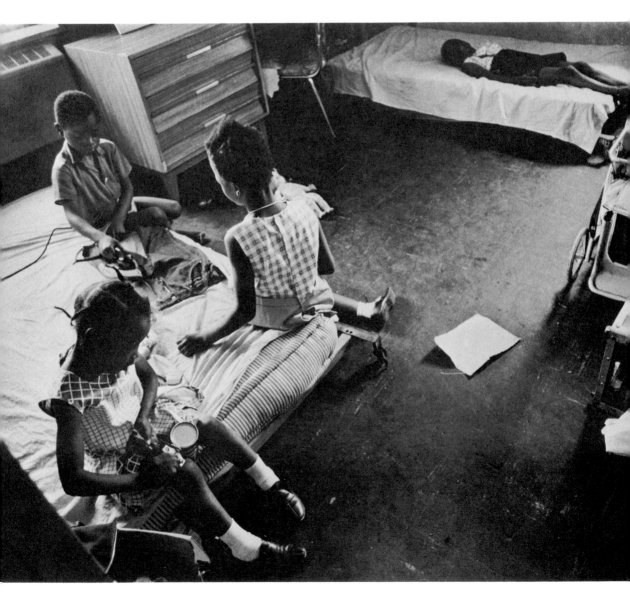

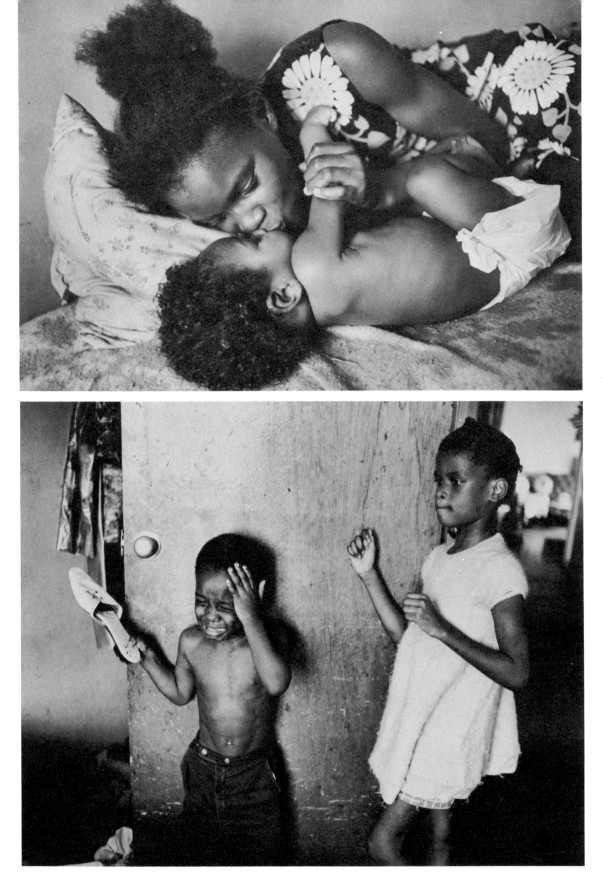

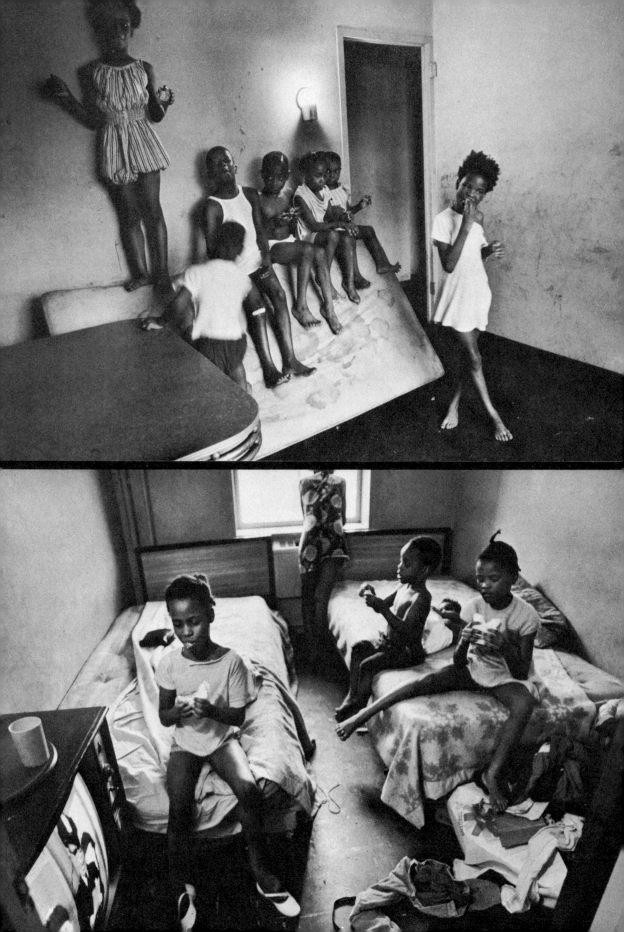

CORINA–six years old

I love God an Frances, cause her is
my mother. I love my daddy. He
like my mother. I like Jesus an the
whole world. I like my house, cause
my house is good.

I like to play toys, doll babies, make
up the beds an clean up.

I wanna be a lady. I wanna have a
father, cause that one left. He got
a girl friend.

I like clean up an play — play toys,
doll babies. I give them bottle.

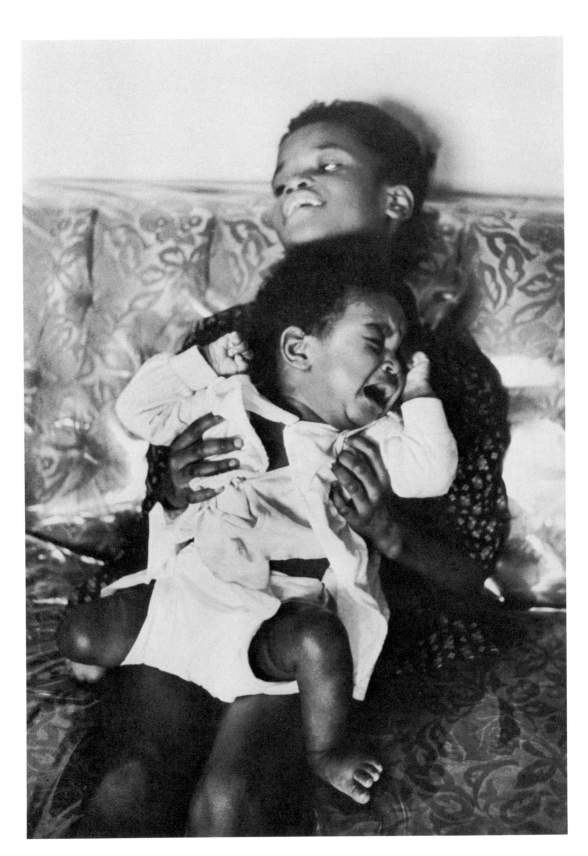

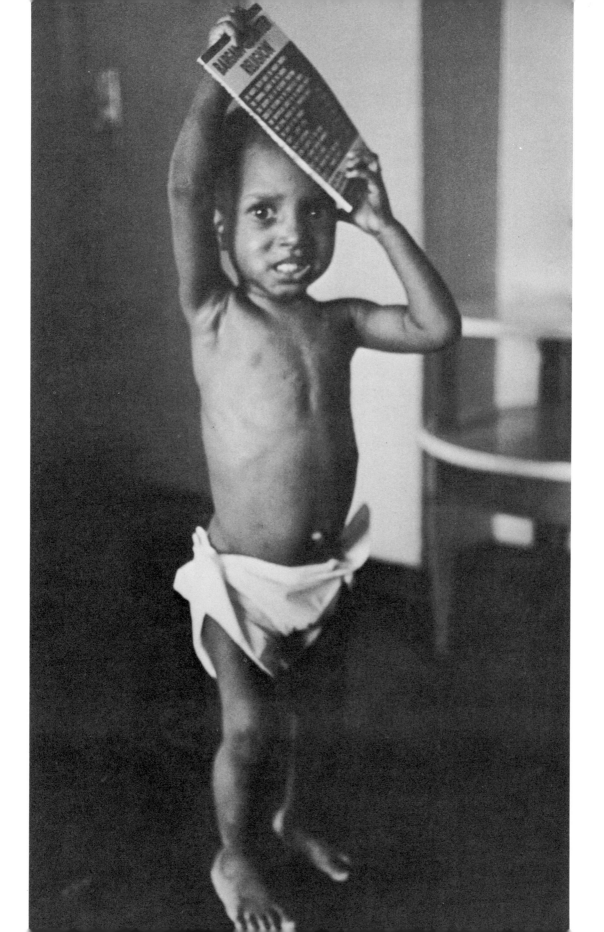

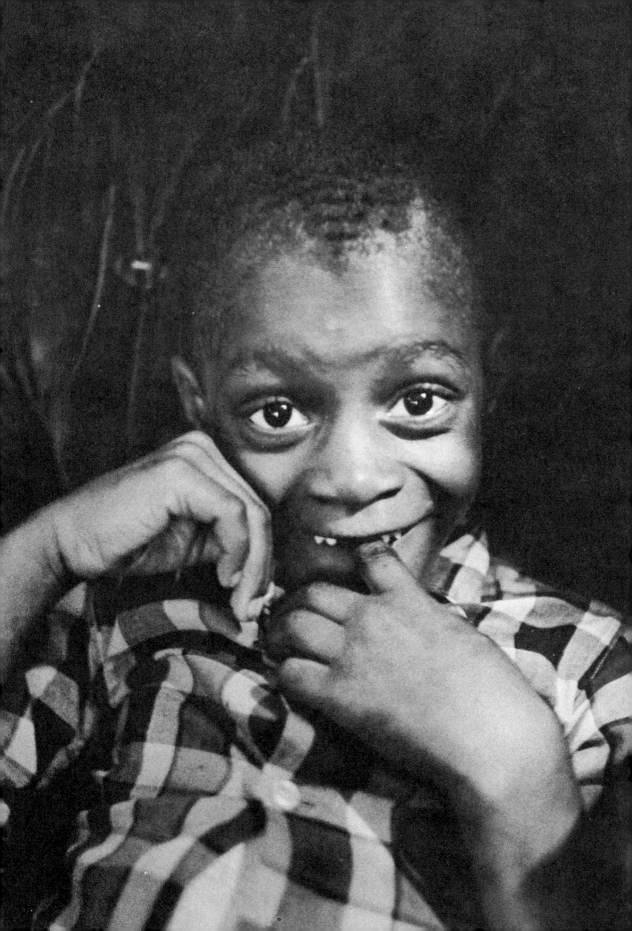

JOE–seven years old

I like to be a cop, cause I want to
help somebody. I wanna be a fireman
too.

I'd like a bike — a big one. I want a
chair. I want a table set. I'd put it
in my room an I'd eat on it. I'd like
to sit down on a chair.

I love Frances, cause she my mother.
Frances taught me about God. She
told us about the Holy Ghost an the
Bible. I know about the Devil. He
give you poison food; if you eat it
you gonna die.

I like to play monster — scare
Michelle an Greta, Michael, Kim.

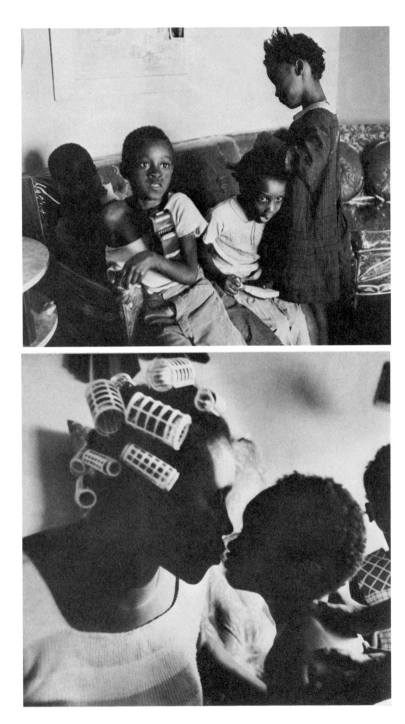

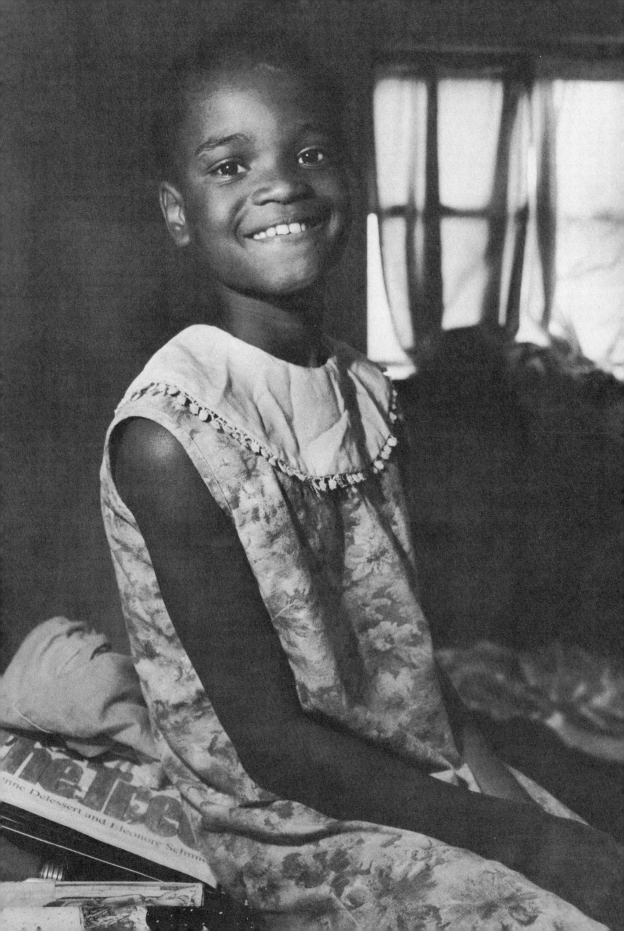

GRETA–eight years old

I want a bed, cause I want to sleep on it. A bed for one people. I sleep with Michelle.

I like my school, cause I like playing there. We play outside in school. I like to go to school. She give us candy.

I want to be a nurse, cause I like being a nurse. When you sick the nurse help you.

My job is to clean up. I sweep an I wash dishes.

I wanna be a lady. I go shoppin an then I go buy clothes.

I like a boat, cause I like to ride in boat. Somebody give me a boat, so I put it in water — a little boat. I take Michelle an Corina for a ride on my big boat. If I get a little boat, I give it to my brother, "Poopie."

I would like a telephone cause somebody promised me for a telephone. Frances promised me for Christmas. But she didn't buy me a telephone for Christmas, she buy Corina a telephone.

I want a bed.

I love Frances the best in the whole world an then I love "Poopie" an I like Corina, an Michelle, an Michael. My father say he gonna take us to the circus. I like my whole family.

I love God an Jesus an Mary. She don't take me to church. My friend Wanita take me to church. She taught me to pray an not to cry when I was sick, cause God gonna make me well. I say my prayers today an every night. I ask God to take care of Michael, an "Poopie," an Joe, an Nathaniel, an Corina an me.

I like to be a mother, because I always like to be a mother, cause I want to stay in the house an clean up —do work. I like to clean up when I grow up. An I like to wash dishes. I like to do so many things.

I wanna be the woman that stops the cars downstairs in the street.

I like to sweep up most. I like to wash dishes more than I sweep up. Have fun makin beds. I like to play, cause I like to have fun an play outside an not in the house. I play tag with my sister Michelle. We play house. I be the mother, you be father, you be child. I be mother. I cook, clean up, dust.

An I want something for Christmas. I want a triangle. I played with it in the nugic [music] room. I like bells too.

I like library. I take books an you bring them to the library an you can change them.

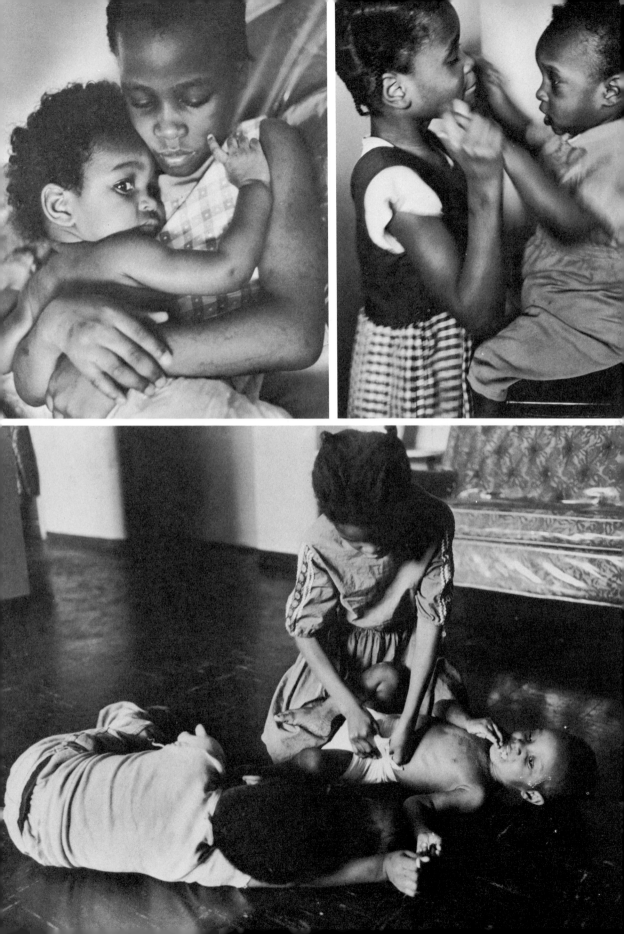

MICHELLE—nine years old

I would like to be a mother when I grow up, because I like to do many things; shoppin, clean up, wash the dishes an sweep up. I want to be a lady and a mother too. I like to be like my mother. I'd like to have children like my mother got. I like five. I like children. I'd teach them how to be smart. I'd teach them how to write an read an spell — so you can learn in school.

Yes I like school, cause I want to learn to read an write an spell, so I can be real smart — so I can't be dumb. Cause I don't want to be dumb.

I like my father to take me to the swimming at the Palisades. I like to see him. I like money from my father; I'd buy me some clothes. I just like a lot of clothes. I like my father and I love him. My father like me. He got another house by hisself. He say one of these days he's gonna take Michael and me an Greta an Kim — he gonna take us to his house. I never saw his house before. He say he was gonna take us out, but he never take us.

I like to play house. One of the boys be father. Father go to work an make money at a job.

I wish for a bike. I wanna take it outside an ride it.

I love God an my mother an my father an my little brother.

I love my whole family.

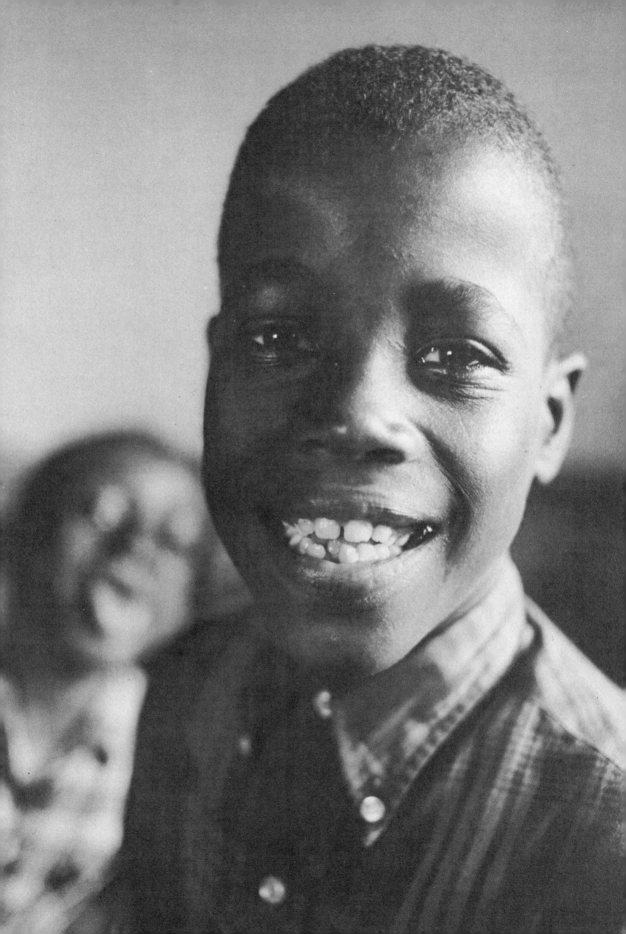

MICHAEL–nine years old

I want a bed.

I wanna be a fireman. I wanna help
people, so I can work.

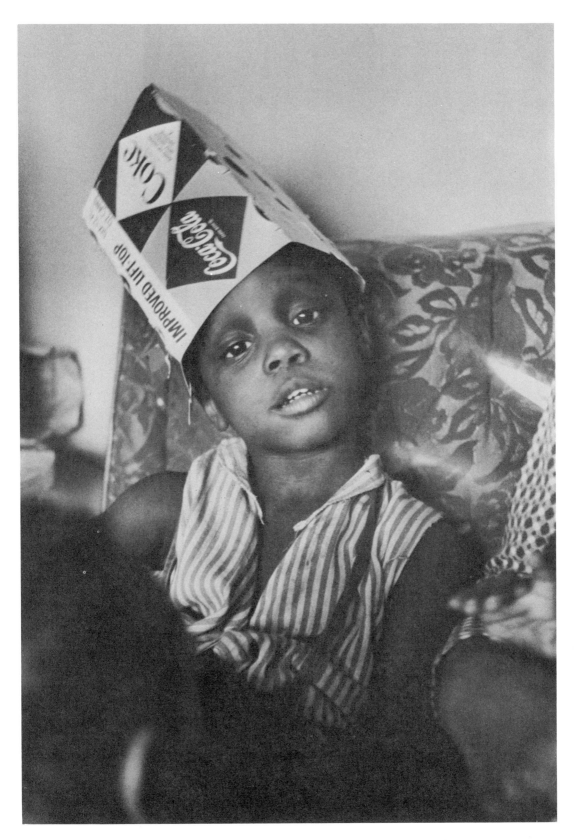

KIM–eleven years old

I love a bicycle an some clothes.

I love my mother because she nice to me. She feeds me. She put clothes on me. She lets me go out. She buys me things.

I love God. He brought me into this world. He nice to the faithful.

I want to go to school till I be in the twelfth grade. Then I go to training school to be a nurse. I like to help people. My mother told me that I should always help people an that I should love them. My mother said that when people does bad, to tell God to help forgive them.

I want somebody to help me if I can't help myself. Like when I need a little training — like being a nurse. I need somebody to be there. When I see that my brothers have cavities, I tell my mother an she take them to the dentist.

We just stay home and look at TV. If there is no day camp, I just go downstairs to play or either upstairs to look at TV. I go to the park an go swimming in the school park. We don't go to 110th Street because there a lot of bad people around.

Sometimes I don't go outside. You know I don't want to be bothered with people that don't want to play. They not used to me around our block. You know I always try to make friends, but they don't want to make friends with me. I hear people say, "You know the Black family bring bad luck." In summer they start beating us up. They just don't like to play with us.

My friends say, "Kim, you get the Welfare food." I say, "Because we want to," an they say, "Kim, you shouldn't get the Welfare." I say, "Sooner or later you gonna be on Welfare too." They shout, "Welfare food, Welfare food." My mother say, Pay no attention to them. They on Welfare, don't you forget it."

First of all I want good clothes for school.

One time I was sick, I stay home a month an I was scared that I was gonna get left back and my mother gonna beat me. She say, "Kim, if you don't get promoted," she say, "Kim, I going to put you away." But I didn't believe it. You know how mothers are. When I get my report card, I was happy. Our whole family was happy they was promoted.

LINDA–thirteen years old

When they see me out in the street an in my school — the kids be lookin out the window because we have pep period, so the kids see all those ladies an they say, "Linda, I see your mother an she gonna get the Welfare food an everything." I say, "You don't see my mother," an they say, "You on Welfare." They ask me who I get my Cons [Converse sneakers], an I tell them, "Don't worry about it." They say, "Your mother get a Welfare check," an I say, "No, my mother don't."

Some of them that talks about me, yeh, they on Welfare. I don't like to tease people on Welfare, cause I'm on it myself. They just makin fun, so everybody can laugh. I feel bad that everybody in school know.

When we first moved here, we didn't have curtains up on the window. We was tryin to get everything together in this house, an they keeps on sayin, "No curtains in the window." An then my sisters happen to come downstairs. They has nice clothes, but they, you know, just dirty up too fast. An then when they dirty up the kid, they say, "Look at them bums, they don't even know how to keep clean!" An when my

sisters an brothers sit on the bench, these boys, they move themselves at where they don't have to sit by them, because they think they stink.

I love the Lord, my mother an my father an my whole family. I like my friends too — sometime, cause they make me mad sometime.

I like to go to the Center after school, play records an we have parties. You have dodge-ball tournaments, punchball tournaments an sometimes we go bowling an ice skating. Sometimes we go to movies an to Palisades. I go there every day, seven o'clock to ten.

I would go outside. I go up to a house an we listen to records.

When my mother had her furniture when we first moved in, I had friends in.

A nurse. I want to help the sick people an help them get well.

The people at school are bad. They take dope. The friends around here, they bad; an I don't want to be about bad kids. They just like to start trouble.

I don't really smoke. I just tries it. They smoke, but their mothers and fathers gives them permission except when they little.

Mrs. Black on
her hopes for the children

I find it best just to raise them and do the best as I can. I don't interfere in no one else's life. Like I don't talk to nobody else about his troubles, you know. Right from wrong, I don't tell them, because we can't talk to everybody.

If I could, I fix the place up decent. Yes the projects themselves are very nice as far as housin concerned, it's very reasonable. Because, I believe, if you had to live somewhere else you wouldn't have as nice a place, as large a place, an the rent be larger than it is. I'd like to buy nice clothes the Welfare doesn't give, nice furniture, clean house, takes them to things I haven't taken them to, like the zoo. I have never taken them to the movies. I'd like once in a while to take them to a restaurant.

I'd make it comfortable for me, like not worrying too much about how my children gonna dress; never what they gonna eat, because most of the time I try to have food in the house. But sometimes I don't know where the next meal is coming from, like when my check be cut. I would try to make it more comfortable for the children. I would try to take them to different libraries an things my kids never seen.

Even I feel like this — regardless what a person do, still I feel I know there's a God. Even though a human bein can be so bad and wrong, that still don't stop one from knowin there's a God. So I preach my children what I believe in, even though I'm not good or right. But, man as a whole, regardless of how he may live, because there's the fact that there's a God — regardless of the fact of how you may live.

I just hope that they be successful. Doctor, lawyer, anything they be, I hope they good at it, anything that they call a honest turn. I want them all to stay in school, but there were times I couldn't send them, cause they didn't have nothin sufficient to wear. Some said they like to be nurses, teachers. I talk to them.

If they can survive just what's goin on out there in the street, I'll be happy for that.

I want them all to be intelligent. I want them to be good human beings. Not everybody that's intelligent is good.

There are honest jobs an jobs that are not honest — illegal jobs. I can't say whether they gonna stay in school. All I can do is hope. In the world today, all we can do is hope.

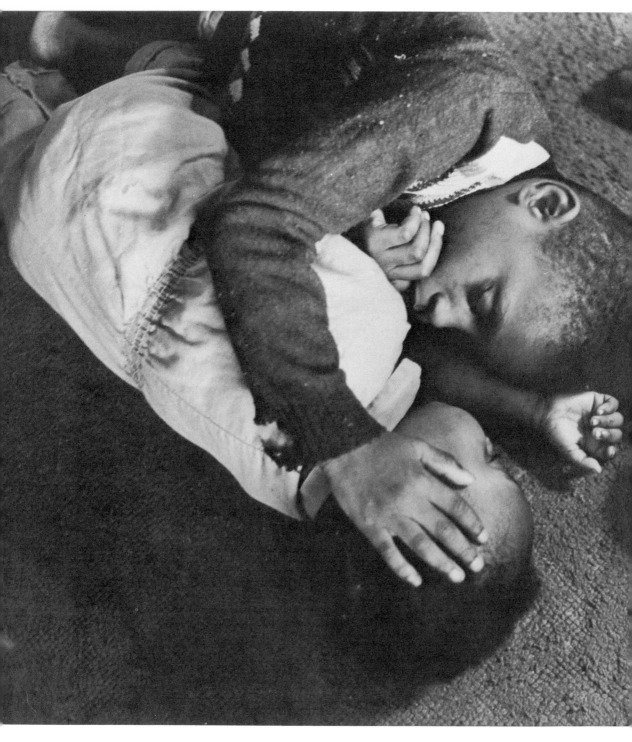

You know, I'm not mean to these
kids. I try to do my best by them.

You know I can have anything I
want as long as it takes children.
I can have my own baseball team,
my own choir, or anything.